OUR
GREAT
STATES

WHAT'S GREAT ABOUT
IDAHO?

✳ Sherra G. Edgar

LERNER PUBLICATIONS ✳ MINNEAPOLIS

CONTENTS

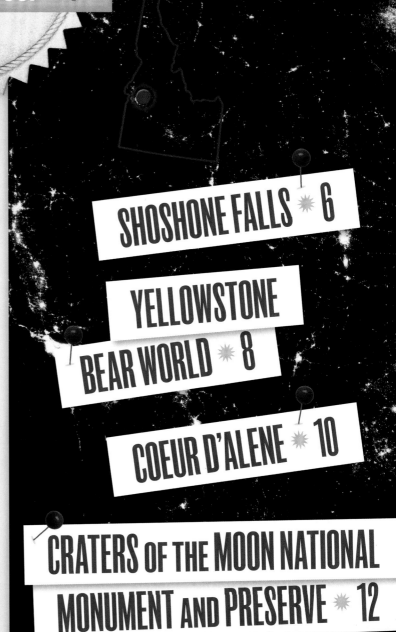

Copyright © 2016
by Lerner Publishing Group, Inc.

Content Consultant: Amy E. Canfield, PhD,
Associate Professor of History, Lewis-Clark
State College

Lerner Publications Company
A division of Lerner Publishing Group, Inc.
241 First Avenue North
Minneapolis, MN 55401 USA

For reading levels and more information, look
up this title at www.lernerbooks.com.

Main body text set in ITC Franklin Gothic Std
Book Condensed 12/15.
Typeface provided by Adobe Systems.

Library of Congress Cataloging-in-Publication
Data

Edgar, Sherra G.
    What's great about Idaho? / by Sherra G.
Edgar.
        pages cm. — (Our great states)
    Includes index.
    Audience: Grades 4–6.
    ISBN 978-1-4677-3881-1 (lb : alk.
paper) — ISBN 978-1-4677-8497-9 (pb :
alk. paper) — ISBN 978-1-4677-8498-6
(EB pdf)
    1. Idaho—Juvenile literature. I. Title.
F746.3.E32 2015
979.6—dc23   2015002510

Manufactured in the United States of America
1 – PC – 7/15/15

IDAHO Welcomes You!

Welcome to the Gem State! Idaho is known as the Gem State because the land is full of gems. Seventy-two types of gemstones come from Idaho. Idaho also has many beautiful valleys and forests to explore. Rivers and streams are open for fishing. Idaho is also the perfect place for winter sports lovers. Snowboard or ski down the state's many snowcapped mountains. If you like to stay indoors, Idaho also offers museums, concerts, and plays. Are you excited yet? Keep reading to learn about ten things you won't want to miss in Idaho!

Explore Idaho's valleys and all the places in between! Just turn the page to find out about THE GEM STATE. >

WASHINGTON

Coeur d'Alene

Saint Joe River

CLEARWATER MOUNTAINS

Lewiston

Snake River

OREGON

MONTANA

Yellowstone National Park

Miles
0 20 40 60 80
0   40   80   120
Kilometers

N

Borah Peak
(12,662 feet/
3,859 m)

Idaho Falls

WYOMING

Meridian

Caldwell Boise

Nampa

Pocatello

Snake River

S N A K E   R I V E R   P L A I N

Twin Falls

UTAH

NEVADA

SHOSHONE FALLS

> Start your Idaho journey just outside the city of Twin Falls. Shoshone Falls is one of the most beautiful sights in Idaho. Water from the Snake River crashes 212 feet (65 meters) into the Snake River Canyon. That is 36 feet (11 m) farther than New York's famous Niagara Falls. Visit the scenic overlook. It's the perfect spot to snap a family photo.

While you're in the area, take a hike and enjoy a picnic. Or go fishing on the Snake River. Then check out Snake River Adventures. Take a relaxing dinner cruise or a speedy jet boat trip. You can also go swimming. Your family will have a ball on this river!

Fish for rainbow trout on the Snake River.

SNAKE RIVER

The Snake River runs through the Pacific Northwest of the United States. This river is 1,078 miles (1,735 kilometers) long. The Snake River begins in the Rocky Mountains. It empties into the Columbia River in Washington State. The Snake River is the biggest tributary of the Columbia River.

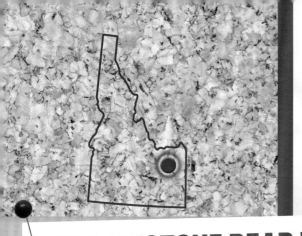

YELLOWSTONE BEAR WORLD

> Be sure to visit Yellowstone Bear World in Rexburg. Drive through the wildlife park in your own family vehicle. You'll see lots of animals up close. Can you spot the elk, bison, deer, goats, moose, American black bears, grizzly bears, and gray wolves that roam the park?

Or travel through the park on a Curator Tour. On this tour, you'll ride on the upper deck of an open truck. Get close to and take pictures of adult bears. You can even feed bears that come up to the truck!

After you're done driving through the park, visit the petting zoo. It covers an area of over 100 acres (40 hectares). Animals roam free in the petting zoo. If you're lucky, maybe you and your family could see deer fawns or elk calves inside the petting zoo! Then go behind the scenes for the most exciting part of Yellowstone Bear World. Join the keepers to pet, hold, and even bottle-feed a bear cub!

YELLOWSTONE BEAR WORLD

BEARS OF YELLOWSTONE'S PAST

See American black bear cubs up close at Yellowstone Bear World.

View moose and other large wildlife from your car as you drive through the wildlife park.

COEUR D'ALENE

More than one million lights make up the Coeur d'Alene Resort Holiday Light Show.

> If you really love the outdoors, Coeur d'Alene is a town you don't want to miss! Coeur d'Alene sits between several lakes. Because of all the water surrounding the town, it's a favorite spot for water sports. During the summer, boating, waterskiing, Jet Skiing, and paddleboarding are popular. Coeur d'Alene is also fun in winter. There are two major ski resorts nearby: the Silver Mountain Resort and the Schweitzer Mountain Resort. The Silver Mountain Resort has an indoor water park that is open all year. Slide down the waterslides in summer or winter.

Enjoy a Lake Coeur d'Alene cruise any time of the year.

Coeur d'Alene is also a great place to spend the winter holidays. The city's Christmas tree lighting ceremony is one of the largest in the United States. The city goes all out for this ceremony. Your family can experience the Journey to the North Pole Holiday Lake Cruise. Then see one of the tallest living Christmas trees. Don't miss the town's amazing fireworks show.

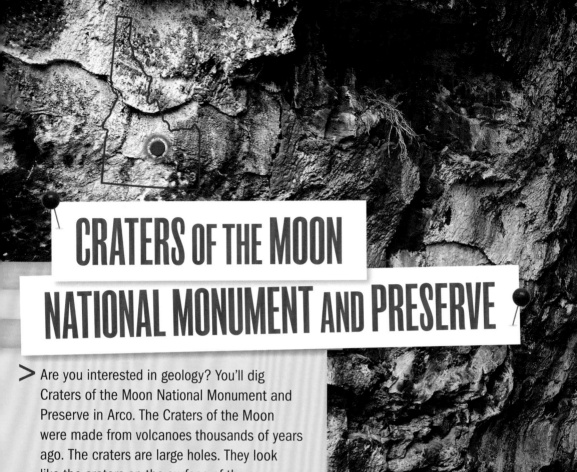

CRATERS OF THE MOON NATIONAL MONUMENT AND PRESERVE

> Are you interested in geology? You'll dig
Craters of the Moon National Monument and
Preserve in Arco. The Craters of the Moon
were made from volcanoes thousands of years
ago. The craters are large holes. They look
like the craters on the surface of the moon.
Visitors can drive through the preserve to see
the craters. Or hike the trails and view them
up close!

More than three hundred caves have been
found in the preserve. Most of them are
lava tubes. Lava tubes are left behind
after some volcanic eruptions. The outside
of the lava hardens as it flows down the
volcano and cools. Then the still-molten
lava inside the tube drains out, leaving a
cave. Climb down rock steps and human-
made staircases to enter Indian Tunnel.
It is a 40-foot-tall (12 m) lava tube.

Explore the 800-foot-long (240 m) Indian Tunnel lava tube.

Hike through unique landscape at Craters of the Moon National Monument and Preserve.

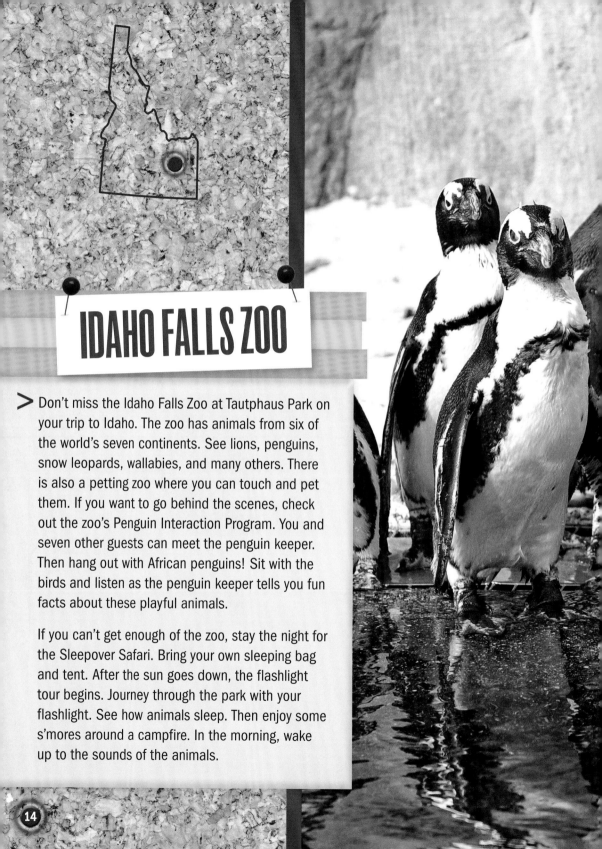

IDAHO FALLS ZOO

> Don't miss the Idaho Falls Zoo at Tautphaus Park on your trip to Idaho. The zoo has animals from six of the world's seven continents. See lions, penguins, snow leopards, wallabies, and many others. There is also a petting zoo where you can touch and pet them. If you want to go behind the scenes, check out the zoo's Penguin Interaction Program. You and seven other guests can meet the penguin keeper. Then hang out with African penguins! Sit with the birds and listen as the penguin keeper tells you fun facts about these playful animals.

If you can't get enough of the zoo, stay the night for the Sleepover Safari. Bring your own sleeping bag and tent. After the sun goes down, the flashlight tour begins. Journey through the park with your flashlight. See how animals sleep. Then enjoy some s'mores around a campfire. In the morning, wake up to the sounds of the animals.

Pet an African penguin and see wallabies from Australia at the Idaho Falls Zoo.

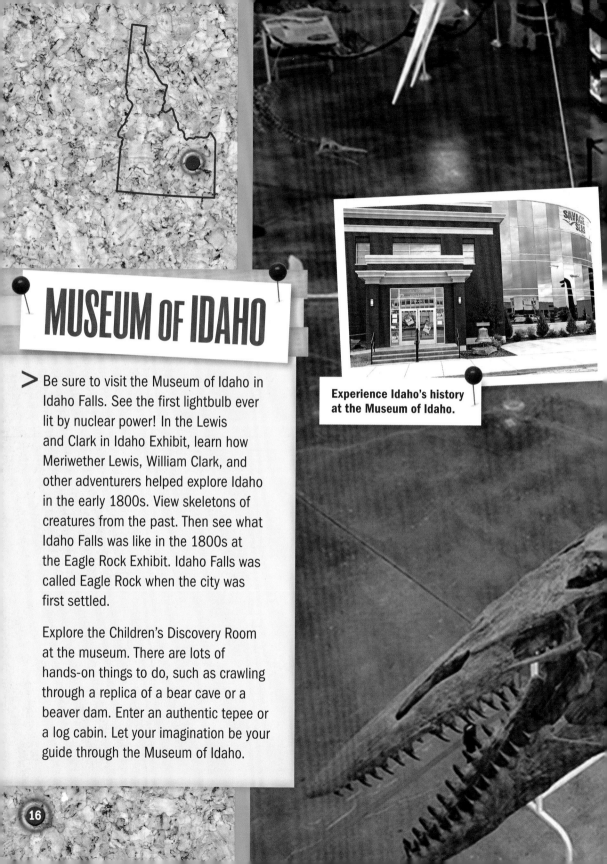

MUSEUM OF IDAHO

> Be sure to visit the Museum of Idaho in Idaho Falls. See the first lightbulb ever lit by nuclear power! In the Lewis and Clark in Idaho Exhibit, learn how Meriwether Lewis, William Clark, and other adventurers helped explore Idaho in the early 1800s. View skeletons of creatures from the past. Then see what Idaho Falls was like in the 1800s at the Eagle Rock Exhibit. Idaho Falls was called Eagle Rock when the city was first settled.

Explore the Children's Discovery Room at the museum. There are lots of hands-on things to do, such as crawling through a replica of a bear cave or a beaver dam. Enter an authentic tepee or a log cabin. Let your imagination be your guide through the Museum of Idaho.

Experience Idaho's history at the Museum of Idaho.

LEWIS AND CLARK

In 1803, President Thomas Jefferson asked Meriwether Lewis, William Clark, and a group of others to explore the territory west of the Mississippi River. Known as the Corps of Discovery, the group traveled from Saint Louis, Missouri, to the Pacific Coast and back. They documented the land, animals, and American Indian tribes they came across. The corps met Sacajawea, a member of the Shoshone American Indian tribe. Sacajawea and the Shoshone tribe helped the corps travel through Idaho and onward to Montana on its way to the Pacific Coast. The journey lasted from May 14, 1804, to September 23, 1806.

Downata Hot Springs offers swimming lessons.

DOWNATA HOT SPRINGS

> Have you ever been to a natural hot spring? Visit Downata Hot Springs in Downey. This outdoor freshwater pool is always warm—no matter how cold the weather is. Each day 234,000 gallons (886,000 liters) of natural hot water flows in and out of the pool. After swimming in the pool, slide down the Dragon Slide and Black Hole tube waterslides. The Black Hole even dips underground for part of the ride!

Downata has several places to stay, including a campground and cabins. Have a picnic near the pool. You can even take swim lessons. You'll have so much fun in the water that you won't want to leave!

HOT SPRINGS

A hot spring is groundwater that is heated by magma below Earth's surface. Water from hot springs is usually much warmer than the surrounding air temperature. The water temperature in a hot spring can range from approximately 102°F to 112°F (39°C to 44°C). Idaho has hot springs throughout the entire state.

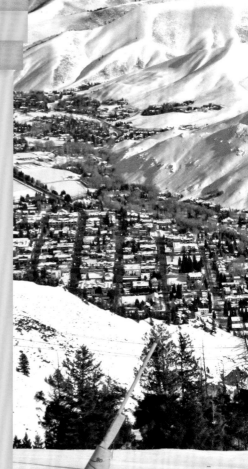

Sun Valley Resort offers great slopes for skiing!

SUN VALLEY RESORT

> Sun Valley Resort in Sun Valley is the most popular ski resort in Idaho. It is known for its great cross-country skiing and snowshoeing. You can also downhill ski and snowboard here. If you're new to these sports, spend some time at the resort's SnowSports School. The instructors offer group or individual lessons so you'll be ready for the slopes. If skiing and snowboarding are not your thing, there are many other activities to enjoy. Some of these include indoor and outdoor ice-skating, snow tubing, and horse-drawn sleigh rides. You can even take in an incredible ice show. Watch as skaters jump and spin on the ice. You'll love the show's music!

Are you visiting in the summer? There's plenty to do without snow too. You can go fishing or horseback riding. Try mountain biking while you're here. Guides will show you how to shift and brake your bike while riding off-trail. Visitors also enjoy tennis and golf. Then catch a movie in an old opera house.

Try snowshoeing
in Sun Valley.

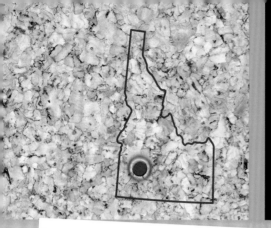

AQUARIUM OF BOISE

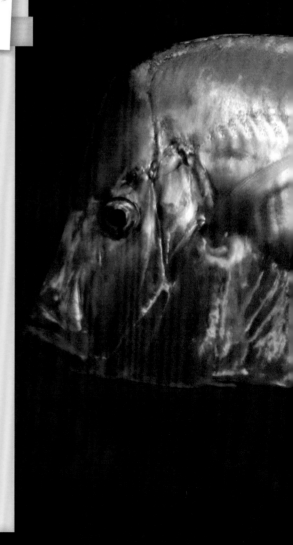

> Travel to Idaho's capital city of Boise. Be sure to stop by the Aquarium of Boise. It's a place you'll never forget. The aquarium is full of exciting exhibits such as the Octopus Palace. The palace includes a 1,200-gallon (4,542-liter) tank for octopuses. See the octopuses up close. Learn about them and their ocean home.

There are more than 250 species of ocean life at the aquarium. Some ocean animals include puffer fish and different types of sharks and stingrays. The aquarium has many hands-on activities too. Would you like to feed or touch a shark or a stingray? The aquarium staff will help you do this safely.

After getting up close with sea animals, check out the Caiman Exhibit. Get a close look at a rare dwarf caiman while listening to fun facts about this animal. Caimans are reptiles similar to alligators. The Aquarium of Boise keeps them in a freshwater pool.

See a giant Pacific octopus—the biggest kind of octopus—at the Aquarium of Boise.

BOISE

Boise has the largest population of any city in Idaho, with around 214,000 people. It is located in southwestern Idaho. The city sits on the banks of the Boise River and is nicknamed the City of Trees because of the many trees surrounding the river.

BRUNEAU DUNES STATE PARK

> Just south of Boise is Bruneau Dunes State Park. Bruneau Dunes is located on miles of sand dunes. The tallest dune in the park is 470 feet (140 m) high! It is the highest dune in North America. You can dune ski, snowboard, or sled on the sand! These sports are just like winter sports but are played on sand instead of snow.

During the summer, ride a horse through the dunes. There's also a 9-mile (14 km) trail around the park for horseback riding. Stay for a few days and camp in the park. While there, be on the lookout for local wildlife, such as coyotes, rabbits, hawks, and herons. Fish and boat on the park's lakes. The Bruneau Dunes Observatory is open during the summer. It is Idaho's largest public observatory. You can view the beautiful night sky through a large telescope.

Make sand angels in the dunes.

You might spot some great horned owls in Bruneau Dunes State Park.

YOUR TOP TEN

You've read about ten things to do and see in Idaho. Now, it's your turn! Think about what your Idaho top ten list would look like. What would you like to see if you were going to Idaho? Do you love activities in the great outdoors? Do you enjoy visiting museums or learning about animals? What sounds most exciting? Keep these things in mind while you make your own top ten list!

IDAHO BY MAP

> MAP KEY

⬡ Capital city

○ City

⬡ Point of interest

▲ Highest elevation

–··– International border

–·– State border

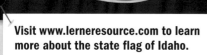

Visit www.lerneresource.com to learn more about the state flag of Idaho.

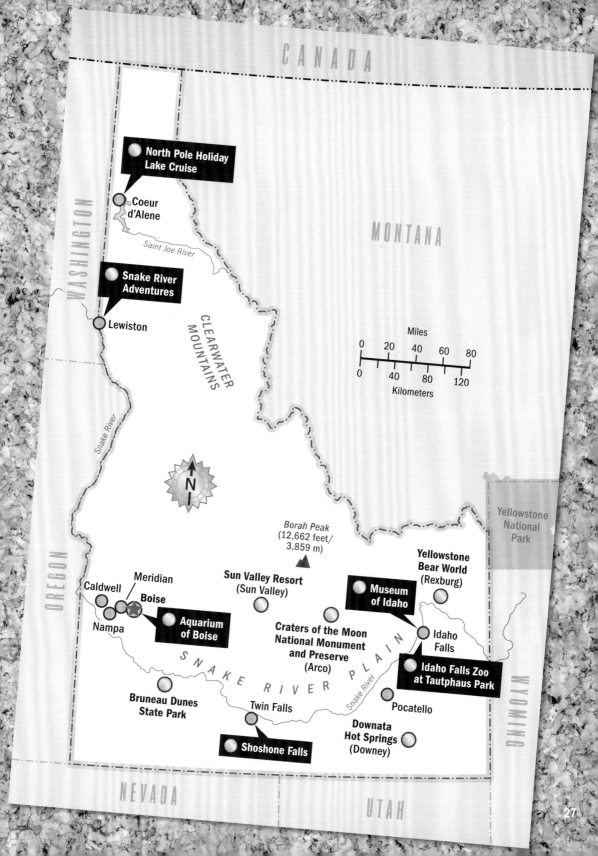

CANADA

MONTANA

North Pole Holiday
Lake Cruise

Coeur
d'Alene

Saint Joe River

WASHINGTON

Snake River
Adventures

Lewiston

CLEARWATER
MOUNTAINS

Miles

0   20   40   60   80

0   40   80   120

Kilometers

Snake River

N

Borah Peak
(12,662 feet/
3,859 m)

Yellowstone
National
Park

OREGON

Sun Valley Resort
(Sun Valley)

Yellowstone
Bear World
(Rexburg)

Meridian

Caldwell   Boise

Museum
of Idaho

Nampa

Aquarium
of Boise

Craters of the Moon
National Monument
and Preserve
(Arco)

Idaho
Falls

Idaho Falls Zoo
at Tautphaus Park

S N A K E   R I V E R   P L A I N

Snake River

Pocatello

WYOMING

Bruneau Dunes
State Park

Twin Falls

Shoshone Falls

Downata
Hot Springs
(Downey)

NEVADA

UTAH

IDAHO FACTS

NICKNAME: The Gem State

SONG: "Here We Have Idaho" by McKinley Helm and Albert J. Tompkins

MOTTO: *Esto Perpetua* (Latin phrase for "Let it be perpetual")

> **FLOWER:** syringa

TREE: western white pine

> **BIRD:** mountain bluebird

ANIMAL: Appaloosa horse

> **FOOD:** potato

DATE AND RANK OF STATEHOOD: July 3, 1890; the 43rd state

> **CAPITAL:** Boise

AREA: 83,569 square miles (216,443 sq. km)

AVERAGE JANUARY TEMPERATURE: 23°F (−5°C)

AVERAGE JULY TEMPERATURE: 67°F (19°C)

POPULATION AND RANK: 1,612,136; 39th (2013)

MAJOR CITIES AND POPULATIONS: Boise (214,237), Nampa (86,518), Meridian (83,596), Idaho Falls (58,292), Pocatello (54,350)

NUMBER OF US CONGRESS MEMBERS: 2 representatives, 2 senators

NUMBER OF ELECTORAL VOTES: 4

NATURAL RESOURCES: cobalt, copper, fossils, gold, lead, precious gems, silver, timber, zinc

AGRICULTURAL PRODUCTS: barley, beef cattle, hay, milk, potatoes, sugar beets, wheat

MANUFACTURED GOODS: computer and electronic equipment, food products, wood products

STATE HOLIDAYS AND CELEBRATIONS: Sacajawea Heritage Days, McCall Winter Carnival

GLOSSARY

canyon: a deep valley, often with a river running through it

crater: a large, bowl-shaped cavity in the ground, normally caused by an explosion or a meteorite

dune: a mound or a ridge of sand or loose rock formed by the wind

geology: the study of Earth

lava: melted rock that comes out of a volcano

magma: hot liquid below or inside Earth's crust, which flows out of a volcano or a crack at Earth's surface as lava and then cools and solidifies to form rock

molten: melted by heat

nuclear power: energy that is created when atoms are split or joined

observatory: a room or a building that houses a telescope and other scientific equipment to study stars, planets, solar systems, and other outer space objects

tributary: a river or a stream flowing into a larger river or lake

LERNER
SOURCE

Expand learning beyond the printed book. Download free, complementary educational resources for this book from our website, www.lerneresource.com.

FURTHER INFORMATION

Aronin, Miriam. *How Many People Traveled the Oregon Trail? And Other Questions about the Trail West*. Minneapolis: Lerner Publications, 2012.
Read more about Idaho's history.

Be Outside: Idaho Children in Nature
http://www.visitidaho.org/children-in-nature/
Read about more events and fun things to explore in Idaho.

Idaho's Capitol for Kids!
http://idahoptv.org/capitoloflight/kids/tour/tour.cfm
Watch a video or click through photos of Idaho's capital.

Idaho State Symbols Games
http://www.learninggamesforkids.com/us_state_games/idaho
Play games to learn more about Idaho's state symbols.

Mead, Maggie. *Exploring the West: Tales of Courage on the Lewis and Clark Expedition*. Egremont, MA: Red Chair Press, 2015.
Learn more about Meriwether Lewis and William Clark and their adventures to explore the West.

Perish, Patrick. *Idaho: The Gem State*. Minneapolis: Bellwether Media, 2014.
Read more about the geography and culture of Idaho.

INDEX

PHOTO ACKNOWLEDGMENTS

The images in this book are used with the permission of: © Robert Crum/Shutterstock Images, p. 1; NASA, pp. 2–3; © American Spirit/Shutterstock Images, p. 4; © Sharon Day/Shutterstock Images, p. 5 (top); © Laura Westlund/Independent Picture Service, pp. 5 (bottom), 27; © Pinchof 2.0 CC 2.0, pp. 6–7; © pu kibun/Shutterstock Images, p. 7 (top); © HES Photography/Shutterstock Images, p. 7 (bottom); © Andre Jenny/Stock Connection Worldwide/Newscom, pp. 8–9, 10 (bottom), 16–17, 16; © BG Smith/Shutterstock Images, p. 9 (left); © Jan Miko/Shutterstock Images, p. 9 (right); © Joel Riner/Quicksilver Photography, pp. 10–11, 10 (top); National Park Service, pp. 12–13, 13 (bottom); © Jerry Hopman/iStockphoto, p. 13 (top); © Jordan Tan/Shutterstock Images, pp. 14–15; © Idaho Falls Zoo at Tautphaus Park, p. 15 (left); © Denja1/iStockphoto, p. 15 (right); © Everett Collection Historical/Alamy, p. 17; © Downata Hot Springs, pp. 18–19, 18 (top); © Mario Bono/Shutterstock Images, p. 18 (bottom); © IDAK/Shutterstock Images, pp. 20–21, 20; © Bruce McKay CC 2.0, p. 21; © Nathan Hall/Aquarium of Boise, pp. 22–23, 23 (top); © Charles Knowles/Shutterstock Images, pp. 23 (bottom), 29 (bottom); © Gregory Johnston/Shutterstock Images, pp. 24–25; © Gina Bringman/Design Pics Inc/Alamy, p. 24; © Garber/Wanderlustimages/NHPA/Photoshot/Newscom, p. 25; © PromesaArtStudio/Shutterstock Images, p. 26; © Lijuan Guo/Shutterstock Images, p. 29 (top); © Steve Byland/Shutterstock Images, p. 29 (middle left); © Somchai Som/Shutterstock Images, p. 29 (middle right).

Front cover: © iStockphoto.com/Jerry Moorman (Shoshone Falls); © Wollertz/Shutterstock.com (snowboarder); © iStockphoto.com/vkbhat (dunes); © Laura Westlund/Independent Picture Service (map); © iStockphoto.com/fpm (seal); © iStockphoto.com/vicm (pushpins); © iStockphoto.com/benz190 (corkboard).